LURE OF THE CASCADURA

Lure of the Cascadura

by

John Lyons

*To May'
Best regards
from John 1/5/90*

Bogle L'Ouverture

First published by Bogle-L'Ouverture Publications Ltd, 1989
with financial assistance from North West Arts.

copyright © John Lyons, 1989

ISBN 0 904 521 48 6

Published by
Bogle-L'Ouverture Publications Ltd
141, Coldershaw Road
Ealing, London W13 9DU

Cover design by John Lyons

Typesetting by An Grianán, Calais
Printed by
Villiers Publications Ltd
London N6 5AH

FOR
Agnès, Cyril, Edouard, Guillaume and Antoine.

CONTENTS

Introduction	viii
Lure of the Cascadura	1
Island Muse	2
Frontside Backside	4
Midday Barataria	6
School Train and Mangrove Crabs	7
A Poem for My Father	8
The Parting	9
Thunder Storm	10
Mango Love	11
Do You Remember?	13
For the Arawaks of Cu-Mucurapo	14
The Carib Bean	15
Possessed	17
Cloud Shadows	18
Limbo	19
Tobago Crabs Come Out to Die	20
Ham Bone and Tidal Waves	21
Godfather's 'Ole Talk'	22
Tobago Days	23
Jumbie Headman	24
Strange Visitor	25
Tobago Twilight	26
The Earlier Bird	28
Granma's Sabbaths	29
Yella George Again	30
Soucouyant	31
'Skin Skin, Yuh Na Know Meh'	38
Weddin Party	34
Midday Rain in Trinidad	35
'Man Ded, Man Dey'	36
Iguana Chase	38
Rosie Weddin Shoes	39

Jourvay	40
Trinidad Carnival	41
Jab Jab	42
A Different Carnival Madness	44
Kite Warding off *Mal Yeux*	45
Home is Weyever Yuh Is	46
Englan No Muddercountry	47
Loss Promise Lan	48
Dey is Kiats an Kiats	49
Sunseeds of Slaves	51
The Black Poet	52
Indoor Plant	53
African Drought	54
Glossary	55

INTRODUCTION

Experience drawn from life in Britain is brief. Prefaced as the lure of the mythical fish, the *Cascadura*, it is Trinidad and Tobago that emerges in this most sensitive recall. Denied and untended landscapes of mind are reclaimed, studied and celebrated. John Lyons' poetry finds a destination from where it looks back, keen in eye, sharp in memory and feeling. A first book by this artist and poet is a book of maturity.

It is a seasoned mas-player who takes you to Carnival. Steel-pan rhythms leap up — lingeringly in the ear. A sensuous life texture becomes a gratifying infectious energy. In the end you return from an enjoyable celebrated excursion.

In 'School Train and Mangrove Crabs' the:
> *Black mangrove mud nyam up frightened baby crabs*
> *when steam train grinds to a stop, pitches a hoot.*

See something from 'Mango Love':
> *'Ah, ah can show yuh wey to get calabash mango*
> *as big as breadfruit',*

and from 'Midday Rain in Trinidad':
> *Den all-of-a-sudden de wind stir-up vex vex;*
> *butterflies like coloured sweetie paper*
> *spinnin wid de leaves an dust;*

Political independence in the Caribbean stirred a new redefinition of the self. An acceptance that a real African continuity is present there has brought its own dimension of cultural aesthetic. African imagery commonly appears now in the art. It stimulates confidence and pride of identity.

See some words from 'Island Muse':
> *I come with my pen*
> *walking the middle of the jumbie midnight road,*
> *hair standing up, heart big in mouth,*
> *clinging to 'our Fathers', 'Lord is my Shepherds',*
> *avoiding dubious pools,*
> *avoiding obeah big foot,*

> *smelling cacajab,*
> *walking backwards through front door.*

The book laments a sad history, in 'For the Arawaks of Cu-Mucurapo':

> *Where are they now,*
> *the Arawaks who discovered Columbus*

and carries on in 'Possessed':

> *After years of nights laden with grief*
> *and tears burning fissures in your face,*
> *you spirited away from your flesh,*
> *slavers' chattel.*

'A Poem for My Father' examines father's peculiar independence:

> *There were some*
> *who thought you learned too easily*
> *to hold your tongue between teeth,*
> *to wear too comfortably in the sun's burning*
> *your three-piece suit.*

Folklore and myths that crop up around the Caribbean in different guises shine out in Trinidad style.

Lure of the Cascadura will settle with the best of Caribbean writing.

James Berry

LURE OF THE CASCADURA

Exiled under silver birch and conifers
I see the poui and immortelles blooming;

the mistle-thrush sings,
but I hear the kiskadee,
>   *Qu'est ce qu'il dit,
>   qu'est ce qu'il dit.*

Blue crabs scuttle in mangrove mud
where this forest floor is a compost
of dead leaves;

that grey squirrel is no agouti
sniffing the air for hunters in rain forest;

I listen to the birch's sigh
and hear distant rain approaching;

pewah and *pomme-arac*
usurp the taste of peach and Cox's pippin;

but I have savoured the cascadura
spiced with legend and must return to die
where the scarlet ibis flame.

ISLAND MUSE

I come with my pen
from Baptist Shouters,
candles burning on the edge of darkness
at the side of the road in limbo,
where repentance sings
in hallelujahs,
in amens,
in the clapping harmony of hymns.

I come with my pen
from the drum, drum
drumming Shango rhythms
in the tent of dancing sacrifices,
in the pulsing blood squirts of cocks' hearts.
From the drum, drum
drumming on calabash-covered chicken,
drumming away death with Yoruba magic.

I come with my pen
walking the middle of the jumbie midnight road,
hair standing up, heart big in mouth,
clinging to 'our Fathers', 'Lord is my Shepherds',
avoiding dubious pools,
avoiding obeah big foot,
smelling cacajab,
walking backwards through front door.

I come with my pen
from where the jumbie 'buds' at midday
hoot, hoot, hoot from sandbox tree
and the dog-wailing death-song
suck the last breath of the ailing;
crapaud hopping into drawing room,
mirrors cracking suddenly,

wind coming from nowhere
blows out pitchoil lamps
and blessed candles.

I come with my pen
from cool green forest
where Papa Bois, bearded with vines,
protects the gouti, lapp and quenk;
where macajuel, like fallen-down tree trunk,
sleeps with belly full of cow.
Where mapepire zanana strikes
the deer-chasing dog,
while cigals trill for rain.

I come with my pen
from where the wily douens,
kidnappers of kiddies under full moon,
faceless, walking forward, backwards into bush;
from where Mama Malade is a naked baby
under midnight street lamp whimpering,
La Diablesse hiding her cow foot
under wide French petticoat,
Soucouyant and Loupgarou, balls of fire,
brightening roof tops before the sucking feasts.

I come long years with my pen
and island hauntings
from where my navel string tree
still grows.

FRONTSIDE BACKSIDE

Frontside,
the usual façade for strangers
and official people carrying briefcases.

From the steps beyond the veranda
they turn away to cross the garden
spread like a wide summer skirt,
printed with red and yellow zinnias, intense marigold;

and beyond the white-washed wooden fence on guard,
they joined the suicidal, hell-bent traffic,
screened with rolling dust of the Eastern Main Road,
going from Port-of-Spain to San Fernando.

Backside,
the other side of things,
reserved for family and good friends:

Cheeky, weakling weeds testing their strength
on the tough, garden sugarcane;

careless stepping stones across the black mud
to the latrine, where the heated shit smell fought
valiantly the statutory DDT,
and beyond this, a wilderness of black sage and Christmas
                                                    bush,
where the wilful, wayward fowls find a nesting place;
but this is mongoose country, and fowls have short memories.

After this pathless waste, the grief-acre of graves
grieving west to the modest railway line with its galvanized halt.

Here on one side of the line, the blue crabs
are banking the mangrove mud at the mouth of their holes;

but beyond this point is the real test of friendship:
The swamp oozes to the desolate sea coast with no ships in
                                                         sight.

MIDDAY BARATARIA

The sun at zenith filched the air.
Zandolies hustled dried leaves for insects.
Cocks crowed the midday hour.

Sunlight on the hot, yellow earth rubbed
the edges of a shadow-cooled burying ground

where the sandbox and silk cotton grew
massive on bodies the breath discarded,
spread an aegis for wandering souls turned jumbies.

In the shuttered noonday darkness
siesta inertia possessed the living like lead.

I braved the sun's stroke,
the giggling douens enticing from the undergrowth,
ventured into marigolds looking for fairies,
found a tiny, tiny shoe.

SCHOOL TRAIN AND MANGROVE CRABS

Black mangrove mud nyam up frightened baby crabs
when steam train grinds to a stop, pitches a hoot.

Tough old blue backs flick up antenna eyes,
tuck in their gundies, crouch low, bubble up saliva.

They grew up blasé with this tired coal burner
flattening big nails into little boys' knife blades.

They know its trundling days are numbered.
It is the *l'école biche* boys with slingshots
they keep their eyes on.

A POEM FOR MY FATHER

You lived a peculiar independence,
you, the progeny of slaves
scarred with a history perpetrated
in killing cane fields.

I watched you,
amazed at your well-mannered poise.

Was this mute rage against them
who offered baubles as gems,
vinegar as water?

There were some
who thought you learned too easily
to hold your tongue between teeth,
to wear too comfortably in the sun's burning
your three-piece suit.

There were others who greeted you
with a conditioned respect:
They looked up to you, called you, sir,
cowed by your cultivated Englishness.

Yet you took no vacations abroad.
You cobbled morning, noon and night,
work was a striding to your grave.
All you bequeathed was the memory
of your ways.

THE PARTING

After all these years
your blood-drained face is still
cradled in coffin mauve.

You look so far away
lying there.

I see black serge suits
– brought out only for lodge and funerals –
startling the white lilies around you,
their death fragrance mixing
with odour of camphored wardrobes.

Eyes are raw red;
father a stranger in his gutteral grief moans;
my brothers and sisters
all toddlers' eyes large with innocence.

This day is veiled with tears
as you leave me for the cold earth,
and I only nine.

THUNDER STORM

Black clouds Papa God's face
across the sky. His eyes,
lightning flash, find me curled
in under-bed darkness
where I hide secrets.

His voice like thunder
cracks the roof top.
'Papa God, He angry wid yuh',
Mama says.

'Forgive meh,
forgive meh;

'I go leave batimamselle alone
to fly in peace in de zinnias;

'I go stop callin Ma Joshua
a old Soucouyant;

'no more rudeness in de dark
behind de door;

'I promise to wash dirt off meh foot,
clean meh teet, say meh prayers
before I go to bed at night;

'forgive meh, Mama,
forgive meh.'

MANGO LOVE

Like a long-legged ibis she came
to cool her feet at the stand-pipe
beside the melting asphalt road.
Washicongs in one hand, in the other
bunched-up dress to red flannel bloomers.

Then Bashwah came, stood away from the dark wetness
spreading around the spluttering stand-pipe,
hair coconut-oiled to porcupine quills,
fingers of one hand crossed behind his back for luck,
in the other, a calabash mango.

Face on fire, heart beating a Hosein rhythm;
he said, 'yuh want a bite?'

She cut her eyes at him, sucked her teeth,
studied cool water cascading down her feet.

'Ah, ah can show yuh wey to get calabash mango
as big as breadfruit', he measured space with his hand.

'Den dat mus be a teeny, weeny baby one', she said,
eye-fixing the mango in his hand.

'Ah ehn tellin lie. An ole Mister Bowlin lan
is a big, big calabash mango tree wid plenty plenty.'

'Lehwe go pick mango den', she said with sudden decision,
stepping away from the stand-pipe.

'Meh name is Bashwah, wat is yuhrs? Ah never see yuh
round here before.'

'Amie Bowlin', she replied scampering away.
Her laughter cut the dry air like a corn bird squark.

DO YOU REMEMBER?

That time when our love startled
the red squirrel in the sugar apple tree?

I came to you; you welcomed me
and passion arched a rainbow with your body.

Your touch was like butterfly wings
goose-pimpling my skin bared for you;

I discovered thrill-paths to secret places,
heard music in your cries.

We rode our rising tide,
lay limp in its ebb.

I started then to tell you
how I kept alive a bluchie's fledgeling
in my shirt, warm against my skin,

but can't remember
if I ever finished that story.

FOR THE ARAWAKS OF CU-MUCURAPO

Where are they now,
the Arawaks who discovered Columbus

blundering West to India
war-dancing to tambourines off Punta Arenal?

Their spirits linger still
in Arawak limbo, a valley in Hispanola.

They move in trees and stones
sepulchring Cu-Mucurapo,

where Sedeno once caught
the frightened white of their eyes in his cannon flash.

Where are they now,
these manioc eaters, children of Jacahuna?

Their middens speak
broken phrases of discarded artifacts,

an Amerindian race
devoured by omnivorous history.

THE CARIB BEAN

The Carib bean
green greed
of the French,
of the English,
of the Dutch,
of the Spaniards.

Staple provisions
for conquistadors
trekking to
El Dorado,
trekking
through
'carne',
carni-
vorous jungle
to Montezuma's
headgear of suns
burning,
burning up,
burning the flesh,
igniting
their gold lust,
acrid odours
all the way
to the courts
of Spain.

Carib bean
fed nations of Europe.
They claimed
it went well with everything,
preferred with Arawaks
roasted in flames

of Carapichaima,
of Cu-Mucurapo,
in the flames
of Arima, Chaguanas
and Couva,
before the slaves,
canned in their oozes,
shipped West,
labelled Yoruba,
Ashanti, Coromantee,
brothers of Cudjoe.

So many died:
Africans,
Amerindians,
currency for
the Carib bean.

POSSESSED

Spirit of my forebears
darkening under silk cotton,
wandering shadows like black smoke
dissolving.

After years of nights laden with grief
and tears burning fissures in your face,
you spirited away from your flesh,
slavers' chattel.

Now you cloud
in unforgotten fields of pain,
no peace, no peace with the weight of your grief;
no refuge,
no refuge in those crowded nether places,
where the grieving hollow sound
blows like a cold wind.

I cry out,
I cry out now;
my hidden wounds weep.
Desire for comfort
is the dead slave in the man.

CLOUD SHADOWS
(For Mamie, my great-grandmother)

Anguish covered up her face
as cloud shadows on burnt out cane fields.

Tears filled up her eyes.
I watched her shrink back into history:
memories raking up her tribe's troubles.

She was fleeing from a fearsome forest:
trees limbed with muskets;
finally trapped with a tangle of eyes
like jumbie beads terrified out of pod
in the hiding bush.

She was herded chained to her trauma
to where the collecting sea waited,
rank with centuries of human misery.

Slavers crammed solid laboured
West to the fierce fields burning where
she sweated and bled with her burden of grief.

And after all this, she survived
though branded beyond the body.

Now, on our coocoo an callaloo Sundays
I watch her drumming Shango rhythms
and cloud shadows drift slowly from her face.

LIMBO

Purgatory of the limbo bar;
limbo, limbo
like souls of slaves
left on the hanging tree.

Hell lends its flames to the limbo bar.

Limbo, limbo
into darkness,
into darkness
to the pulse of limbo music:
the foot-fall rhythms of slaves
leaving their bodies on the hanging tree

to limbo, to limbo
where they still wait for freedom.

TOBAGO CRABS COME OUT TO DIE

That night's moon, the colour of mouse-trap cheese,
was fuller than full moon in rainy season.

Heavy clouds dissolved into sheets of water washing
                                            Scarborough;
the moon was left a clear run of sky.

From every secret, muddy place they scurried sideways,
brandishing the earth's rankness like a shield
too fragile to protect them from the human fear
their superior numbers generated.

I still ask myself,
why did the crabs come out to die?

HAM BONE AND TIDAL WAVES

Sun was shining while thunder rolling;
the devil and his wife was 'cussin'
and fighting over a ham bone.

They broke open the sky
'wid dey pushin an dey shovin',
and the rain poured down
on Rockley Vale,
on the cashew tree
in front of Granma's house,
where a yellow pool spread,
where Bat-ears Elton tested pool water
for barracudas with jigger toes:
Mango-head Winston harpooned
earthworm monsters floundering in shallows;
Yampee-eye Nevil wanted an ocean
with cashew leaves armada,
bush bug swashbuckling English buccaneers.

But Know-it-all Winifred,
the devil's favourite girl child,
came splashing,
made tidal waves.

GODFATHER'S 'OLE TALK'

Everybody called him Godfather.
I once saw a portrait by Cézanne
of an old man just like him,
dappled with the colours of permanent summer.

Godfather sat at ease with his garnished tales:
how once he played cricket with Edward,
the Prince of Wales, when they were both young
and agile on a pitch in Tobago,
now somebody's sweet potato patch.

The memory of those gone days
passed through him like an earth's tremor,
and his eyes for a brief moment
lit up like a candlefly's.

He seemed glad for my company
and the present of Vat 19 rum from Trinidad.
He cried a little.

TOBAGO DAYS

Where I played
a forest of suffering once grew.
'Black Jacobins' in chains
were brought there long ago.

Amidst bush and bramble
I grew wild as rocksage, learned
how to avoid stepping on snakes.

I taunted squirrels:
ate mangoes on their stems,
braved pikant patch for gri-gri,
got bunged up with guava seeds;

roasted breadfruit on bleached stones
where rivers flowed in rainy seasons,
cracked open coconuts hard as rock,
raked stagnant pools for crayfish.

But these were my gallivanting
Saturdays and holidays.
Sundays were real sabbaths:
Sunday school with cousin Cecille
and after-lunch siestas.

Weekdays after school were a burden
of chores: With hoe and rake
I bullied the soil between cassava beds,
toted firewood on head pad,
filled water barrels while I hastened
the night with hard wishing.

JUMBIE HEADMAN
(The announcer of death)

He lived unapproachable
at the heart of his stench;

armed with sharp thrust of eyes,
cutlass cradled in the crook of his arm.

With the brash obscenity of a carrion crow
he savoured the smell of death.

Before jumbie birds hooted,
before the *crapaud* in the drawing room,
before dogs howled at invisible presences,
before the mirror cracked on the wall,
this announcer of death came in the night,
'Wake people, wake! Wake people, wake!'

Three nights' walk away,
someone had died only seconds ago.

STRANGE VISITOR

I have seen you often coming
out of earth and trees,
feet with callous armour
against the jooking pikant.

Hands, thick fingers
permanently crippled
to a semblance of elegance
for Granma's best china cup
of sweet soursop tea.

Sweat-stained, the immutable
khaki shirt and baggy trousers,
strengthened at points of frazzle
with grease-fixed grime, held carelessly up
by broad leather belt.

What cynical paralysis fixed
that illegible expression on your midnight face?
With whom did you seal conspiracies of reticence?

Once when Granma had a shivering *maladie*,
you came to her disguised in medicinal herbs;
but I knew you by your armoured feet.
You disappeared into Granma's bedroom behind locked door.
Odours of another world filled the curious silence.

That was the last I saw of you.
Granma got better, though.

TOBAGO TWILIGHT

The sun mellows like old Godfather,
softens definitions of shadows
that pass over everything in their path.

Sheep and goats come in from pasture,
sit in the murk under-house,
masticate their day's cuds.

In the garden a king of the forest
glides to a low branch of a mango tree,
hoots royally at the gathering dark, flies off.

Mosquitoes are being smoked out of the house
with burning herbs before nets are dropped over beds.

Fruit bats circle around sapodilla trees,
coming head on, but never colliding.
There are plenty bat-bitten sapodillas for morning.

The last bucket of water is being drawn
from the stand-pipe beside the road
to fill water barrels for next day's washing.

Dick, the red Rhode Island cock, leads his hens
up makeshift ladders to the plum tree roost.

Then it is time to sit around table on rough-hewn benches,
to eat slices of johnny-bakes daubed with salty,
orange-coloured margarine, drink herb tea,

and after, to do our sums or read silently
under threat of Tom Stickley, the harness leather strap
rigid in Granma's lap.

Soon she will be singing 'Rock of Ages'
in her thin inimitable voice, stopping
frequently in mid note to malign her neighbour
of many-years feuding. She calls him Polyphemus.

He would glare into the gloom at our house,
from his side of the cactus fence, singing
godless songs loud enough for her to hear.

Soon we will be saying good night to Granma.
She is sitting on her tired stool, toothless with
blunt knife scraping the last pulp from a mango seed.

Soon night shadows will stain everything
like black ink. Candleflies will glow intermittently
in flight; crickets and frogs will take their cue
from the star-sprayed sky to play their nocturne
and our lullaby.

THE EARLIER BIRD

In de season wen mango smell sweet sweet,
wen sapodillas drop down easy,
an nite rain poun galvanize roof hard,
I go to bed wishin fuh foreday mornin to come.

Nite rain always mek plenty fruit fall down;
buh yuh have to get up before gol-eye sarah,
fuh she, earthworm was secon bess to sapodilla.

Meh cousin Yvonne was a earlier bird though:
Sometimes she tek de wrong step tip-toin
an de floor boards creak me outa meh sleep
to see she vanishin tru back door.

I only secons behine she, buh ah still too late;
she already under de sapodilla tree
leggy as a god-horse, dress tail bunch up
full of fruit in front she.

I tellin yuh, I wasn't stayin dey
to pick up no half-eat-up sapodilla
she lef on de groun;
me, I head fuh de mango tree.

Afterwards wen day clean,
we exchange small mangoes fuh small sapodillas,
buh wid no bat bites.

GRANMA'S SABBATHS

Woe to the breakers
of Granma's hymn-singing sabbaths,
to blasphemers of her God-spell
cast to silence the wind's pea-pod rattling,
'bluchies' chattering in the hog plum tree,
cackling gol-eye sarah.

Granma's sabbaths,
always a sit-down breakfast:
cocoa tea, fry bakes and saltfish accra.

After breakfast, the clean-starched-linen-smell march
from Rockley Vale to any church in Scarborough.

'Dey's only one Gaard, and chuh is chuh,
praise de Laard', Granma used to say.

Then after service, Sunday school bible tales:
'Jonas in de whale belly, Daniel in de lion den'.

No work on sabbath day, but no play either.
'Johnieeeeeeee, hall yuh tail ere;
how many tim es ah tell yuh not to play
"stick-em-up" on de Laard sabbath.
Johnieeeeeeee, wey yu dey, comere yuh little vagabon,
yuh come right ere befoe ah whip yuh backside
till it black an blue!'

YELLA GEORGE AGAIN
(Granma's coocoo)

Yella George wid corned fish
stewed wid coconut.

Yella George wid dasheen leaf callaloo
an a piece ah salt beef fuh flavour.

Yella George sure to full up hungry hole.

Buh take what I tellin yuh,
dohn love Yella George too much,
or he go lie doun heavy on yuh belly
an yuh go have to wash him doun wid bush tea;

an if dat dohn work,
senna pods sure to flush him out good.

Grine de carn bwoi, grine de carn fuh mek Yella George
to give yuh strent to grine moe carn.

SOUCOUYANT

Look dey!
Dat big big ball-a-fire
on ole Gaskin roof top.

Oh Gaard, oh Gaard!
Is Soucouyant.
Quick man,
run before she see we.

Ole Gaskin go wake up
in de marnin he skin
black and blue
wey Soucouyant suck im;

ah tellin yuh,
he blood must be sweet,
cause ah hear
she suck im aready.

Many times I tell im
to mark crosses, X's an noughts
on he winda an doors
to stop Soucouyant
from suckin im;

or pile a heap a rice
on he doorstep
fuh Soucouyant to count,

buh man, he stubborn
like a ole jackass,
yuh tink he listenin to me.

Yuh know wah dem people sayin,

Ma Mable who livin doun de road
in dat rusty galvanize shack
is a Soucouyant.

Is true, ah tellin yuh.
I see she aready wen she tun round,
cussin and lashin out wid she poui
wen dem ragamuffins in shut-tail
mark a chalk line across de road
wey she walkin.

Come man, dohn stan dey
wid yuh mout wide open
ketchin flies,
leh we run quick
before she see we.

'SKIN SKIN, YUH NA KNOW MEH'

Soucouyant, Soucouyant,
ball of fire vampiring through the night,
I found your skin beneath a water barrel
        and salted it,
        and salted it;

        'Skin skin, is me, yuh na know meh,
        skin skin, yuh na know meh'.

No more banquets of blood,
no more purple rings
on my skin in the mornings;
no more chalk marks: crosses and noughts
on doors and windows to keep you away;
I found your skin beneath a water barrel
        and salted it,
        and salted it;

        'Skin skin, is me, yuh na know meh,
        skin skin, yuh na know meh'.

In daylight, you, an old woman leaning on stick,
shunned the chalk line across your path;
you raved and cursed
marking your next victim with blaze of your eyes.
Children taunted you:
        'Soucouyant, Soucouyant!'
But I found your skin beneath a water barrel
        and salted it,
        and salted it;

        'Skin skin, is me, yuh na know meh,
        skin skin, yuh an know meh'.

WEDDIN PARTY

Tonite Soucouyant and Loupgarou get married
burying groun jumbies sing 'here comes the bride';
jumbie birds come from far and wide,
Papa Bois, La Diablesse,
— an we know how dem two like commesse —
all dem little moonlight douens,
in fact, de whole damn ban
join in de bacchanal.

Even Bacoo-Man come out he little bottle
and fly in from Guyana.

Soucouyant and Loupgarou so happy,
fuh a joke dey conspire
to join up dey ball-a-fire
an nite turn day,
jumbie music begin to play
an everybody dance a breakaway.

MIDDAY RAIN IN TRINIDAD

I

De sun stingin meh skin,
ah sweatin like a horse in de heat.
Palm trees tense up: fraid to move.

High, high up in de sky
ah see clouds: black ink on blottin paper spreading.
Corbeau: tiny, tiny dark specks flying round,
as doh deh tauntin de rain to fall down.

Den all-of-a-sudden de wind stir-up vex vex;
butterflies like coloured sweetie paper
spinnin wid de leaves an dust;

allabout pickney screamin,
'rain, rain, go to Spain an dohn com back again'.

But dat didn't mek no difference:
de rain pelt down hard like gravel.

II

An wen de rain stop fallin,
all tings bright and beautiful,
as meh mudder used to sing.
Meh head reelin wid de sweet, sweet smell risin.
Everywhere ah hear de earth suckin up de water;
gutters in de street full and swift.
Trees twinklin all over wid drops of rain.
Sky clean blue wid no *corbeau*.

'MAN DED, MAN DEY'

Before Boysie gone an get hiself
knock down by a macktruck,
he livin in de rumshop
all day Gord sen.

An wen sun climb down
behind dem mango tree,
he come home stink a rum,
singin at de top of 'is voice:
'ain't no hidin place down 'ere',
he so drunk, he cahn get 'is clothes off.
Buh ah tellin yuh, meh dere,
now he gone away,
man ded, man dey.

An chile, dat's not all:
He always climbin all over meh,
'is ting all wrinkle-up,
hangin down like dem dry banana leaf,
not even a stiff dose of *bois brande*
could mek it stan up;
Oh Gord! Now Boysie gone away,
girl, man ded, man dey.

I give im a good wake, yuh know:
a-lot-a soda biscuits an coffee,
rum was flowin like water,
we sing plenty hymns, especially
'is favourite: 'Abide wid me'.

It was in de wake 'is pardner, Broko,
start givin meh de sweet-eye.
Well, chile, it didn't tek long,
now ah know wat I was missin.

Boysie gone away,
buh man ded, man dey.
We gettin married nex Easter,
before de chile born.

IGUANA CHASE

Iguana, iguana!
Bungalows, ajoupas
spilling out
people milling round
like dried leaves
in gust of wind.

Iguana, iguana!
Pots boiling over
boiling down
rice-an-peas charring
to bu'n bu'n.

Iguana, iguana!
Wey it gone, wey it gone!
over dey, over dey!
Bulldozer bodies
crashing down bush
crushing down fence
bare feet ploughing up
potato patch
cassava beds.

Iguana, iguana!
Dey it go, dey it go!
Yuh na see it
yuh na see it
yuh na see wey it go.

ROSIE WEDDIN SHOES

Rosie new weddin shoes;
like yam fit naygar mout.

After Rosie get married
every year weddin shoes
tun christ'nin shoes;
four years, four pickney.

Wen dey mash doun,
Rosie drag dem like sabot.

Dey on dung heap now,
near wey dem yams grow.

JOURVAY

Foreday mornin
just round de corner.
Steelban
trobbin, trobbin,
trobbin in meh heart
beatin, beatin,
beatin in meh blood;

everybody winin-up,
jumpin, jumpin,
jumpin-up,
bottom to bottom,
breasts to chests,
belly to belly,
hands up down sideways,
all over de place;

and people sweatin,
sweatin fuh so,
waitin, waitin fuh six o'clock.
And when he cock crow on Lavantie Hill
and church bell ring,
ring, ringin out,
Jourvay break away.

We move out on de road,
and pan sweet sweet, ah tellin yuh;
everytin shakin, shakin,
shakin wid de riddum.
JOURVAY!

TRINIDAD CARNIVAL

Di-dong dong, carnival,
dance people in de street,
daah dah-dah, BACCHANAL!

Is Trinidad festival,
listen to calypso beat;
di-dong dong, carnival;

kaiso! kaiso! shake it all,
love, people in de street,
daah dah-dah, BACCHANAL!

Plenty talent musical
playin de steelban beat,
di-dong dong, carnival;

jerk yuh waist, hug yuh pal,
drink yuh rum, chip yuh feet,
daah dah-dah, BACCHANAL!

Maas in yuh maas sensational,
di-dong dong, carnival,
daah dah-dah, BACCHANAL.

CARNIVAL

Oh Gaard! Oh Gaard!
Pan sweet, sweet yuh hear;
LISTEN, LISTEN
to dat beat:
Biddin-ki-diggidin, biddin-ki-diggidin
biddin-ki-diggidin, biddin-ki-diggidin.

Oh a feelin it, a feelin it,
down to the bottom ah me soul.

Hey Doris gial,
I like how yuh movin yuh body,
shake it, gial shake it
CARNIVAL!

JAB JAB

Out of masquerading crowds
they come shuffle-dancing.
Jester-clowns in brilliant satin,
armoured against the lashing whip:
stuffed up like bobolee.
Black face in white face wire mask.
Arms circle in air, whips flash,
crack like gunshots:

We are the boys, jab jab,
from Fyzabad, jab jab,
we fraid nobody, jab jab,
we big and bad, jab jab,
lookin fuh trouble, jab jab,
in Port-of-Spain, jab jab,
we ready an able, jab jab,
so think again, jab jab,
if yuh want to fight, jab jab,
you have no chance, jab jab,
against our might, jab jab,
so shift yuh stance, jab jab,
find yuh money, jab jab,
prepare to pay, jab jab,
or everybody, jab jab,
will rue de day, jab jab,
an only den, jab jab,
I'll go away, jab jab,
jingle jingle, jab jab,
jingle jingle, jab jab,
jingle jingle, jab jab.

A DIFFERENT CARNIVAL MADNESS

Jeez-an-ages, Matilda,
yuh wuds sting meh like zootie,
dey like bitter cassava poisoning meh.

I still yuh man, Matilda;
dohn hold yuhself so tight-tight na.

I promise:
I go stop puttin on yuh pink satin dress
wid de slits doun de sides,
yuh two-tone high heels,
yuh bess earrings,
yuh lipstick an rouge.

I go stop mekin meself a pappyshow,
talkin in meh macumere voice
an limin like a jamette
outside de rumshop on Charlotte Street.

I go stop shoutin, 'maas, maas, play maas',
an tinkin everyday is carnival day;

buh Matilda, ah cahn help it,
I still hear pan beatin in meh head,
an ah tellin yuh, ah ehn mad.

KITE WARDING OFF *MAL YEUX*

I know from my hovering height
there is something more to me
than my pretty cut of colours.

I rose on a wind not strong enough
to ruffle duck's down.

Now I feel your heart beat through taut thread,
your desire to ride with me on the wind's supple strength.

I am your will curved in 'coki-yea' bow and shaft,
squared in green and yellow tissue paper.

I changed your perspective at my height
warding off *mal yeux* with my aerial eye.

HOME IS WEYEVER YUH IS

Well, ah lan up in Englan,
Victoria Station, London.
D I S M A L !
Ah didn't hear no,
'Wahappenin dey, man',
no huggin, no kissin,
no glad-glad cryin.

Englan shockin, *oui*:
sun here ehn no blazin fire
like back home
strong enough to bun people;
here dey so white-white,

an meh skin so black,
black like coocoo pot bu'n bu'n,
still smoulderin
wid sunfire dey cole looks
cahn douse down.

Ah feel so homesick, brodda,
yuh ehn goin believe dis:
Di good Laard come to meh,
an he point to de groun an say,

'Dirt same colour as Trinidad dirt,
it mek same grave fuh white man
as it mek fuh Black man.'

Well, ah tellin yuh, at dis point
ah kneel doun an ah kiss de dirt,
an ah shout out:
'Mamma eart, protek meh,
home is weyever yuh is.'

ENGLAN NO MUDDERCOUNTRY

Englan no muddercountry.
Ole West Indian 'istry book
was tellin lie: is white man
mamaguy.

Englan
no 'Land of Hope and Glory',
ask di so-called Black minority,
dey tell yuh a different story:

buh Englan
'Mother of the Free',
yeh, free to burn a Pak,
free to mug a Black,
is a fack.

Man, dis is National Front country,
wid aerosol-can graffiti:
'Gas the Blacks',
say di writin on di wall.

Here any Black man carry
di collective identity:
wog, nigger, alien disgrace,
slum-maker, wife-stealer,
contaminator of di English race,
job-tief, sociological case,

an yu tellin meh
Englan mi muddercountry.
Cheups!!

Winning poem, 2nd prize Cultureword, 1987.

LOSS PROMISE LAN

Laard, Laard,
wah ah goin do now.
Look at me crosses.
Tell meh wey ah went wrong, meh Laard,
to en up in dis place.

Oh Laard ah fright'n
an feel so expose;
if yeye could knock meh doun ded,
ah would-a-be ded long time.

Wey ah doin in dis country, Laard?
Dey ehn no sun here to write home bout,
to top it all, meh skin gettin pale
ah tellin yuh, ah dohn feel right.

Dis ehn no Canaan lan, Laard,
Yam, eddoes, dasheen an sweet potato
dohn grow in back giard'n.
An ah cahn believe meh yeye,
here in Englan calaloo come in tin.

Yuh cahn go doun in de bush
after de rain stop fallin to pick up ripe mango.

Laard, Laard ah must-a-been blind:
back home in Tobago ah was livin all dat time
in de promise lan, right before meh eyeball
an ah didn't see it.

DEY IS KIATS AN KIATS

Kiats in Englan!
Dey spoil, *oui*:
dey laugh an play
hide-an-seek wid mice;
buh lehme tell yuh someting,
in de Caribbean,
we different altogedder.

Frastart, we always hungry
- as real kiats should be.
Wen we huntin,
we fass like lightnin
ready fuh anyting dat move.

On de odderhan,
here in Englan kiat get fat
on tin food from supermarkit;
man, dey losin all selfrespeck:
dey dohn even begin to know
how to ketch mice;
an dey ha de brassface to believe
dey better dan we back home.

Yuh know wat I tink!
- I go tell yuh anyway -
because dey go to dem beauty salon
to get deself dollsup,
because dey geh deself sterelise,
dey tink dey modern an liberated,
eh heh, ah know wah ah talkin bout
ah tellin yuh,

I hear dem wid meh own ears:
dey call we Caribbean kiats,

'primitive wild beasts',
well, dat mek meh laugh;
we so-called wild beasts
dohn en up in de vet all de time,
we live natural and healty,
free as a bird;
well, free anyway.

SUNSEEDS OF SLAVES

The new sunseeds of slaves
sprouting up through rubble
in England's cityscapes.

In this city's bush
no navel strings are buried;

no sufferings eased
by sighing bamboo grove.

Lost are earth's wisdoms
passed through fingers
familiar with yams and tania
in carib soil.

Across the generation gap
they pelt words like stones
against living brow-bone;

but theirs is a more urgent pain.

THE BLACK POET

Black,
without camouflage
where the car
-nivorous 'pandas' run.

We are the hunted
by un-natural selection.

We learn to fashion
weapons of wit in poetry:

No subtle, diplomatic metaphors;
no hypocritical similes,
but hard, sharp antonyms
of confrontation
expressed in
black and white.

INDOOR PLANT

The spotlight strikes you hard.
Your fleshy green tongues of leaves make
shadows like splodges of black ink on the floor.

Short, bent over like an old oriental,
you could be mistaken for a bonsai tree
not committed to a definitive direction of growth:

yet in spite of your appearance,
the more discerning or kindly disposed
can detect in your sedentary, pot-bound existence
latent desires to be decorative.

Let us dispense with the botanical euphemism
commonly expressed as, 'hardiness'. You are
a typical house plant of the crass variety.
It beats me how you can survive in your
microcosm of arid waste.

AFRICAN DROUGHT

The sun came down,
furnaced the air,
severed clean
the cycle of seasons
with its blade of flame,
coloured everything
a scorched brown,
imposed stillness
as a burden;

life lingers
in frames of bone,
in hanging garments of flesh,
in the inscrutable
depths of eyes.

Nearby on dead trees,
the obscenity of patient crows
waiting,
waiting.

GLOSSARY

ajoupa	a small thatched house.
bacchanal	any large, noisy party; scandal; confusion.
Bacoo-Man	folk spirit from Guyana, like Genie in the bottle.
bloomers	knickers or panties.
bluchie	a blue bird.
bobolee	an effigy or ragdoll representing Judas in a Good Friday ritual.
bois brande	a tree the bark of which is used to make a potion reputed to be an aphrodisiac. Effects last according to dosage.
brassface	shameless audacity.
breakaway	a wild dance.
bu'n bu'n	the burnt part of cooking that sticks to the bottom of the pot.
bush tea	a hot drink made from locally-grown herbs.
bwoi	boy.
cacajab	a magic concoction which when burnt gives off a nauseating odour.
caarn	dried maize.
candleflies	a night beetle whose eyes emit an intermittent phosphorescent glow.
cascadura	a freshwater armoured catfish found in Trinidad. It is said that anyone who has eaten this fish must return to Trinidad to die.
'cheups'	the noise of sucking closed teeth, expressing annoyance.
cigals	cicadas.
commesse	a noisy party, sometimes quarrelsome.
coocoo & callaloo	a much-favoured spicy dish of African origin. It is made with okras (sometimes called lady fingers) and the leaves of the dasheen plant or spinach. See dasheen.

crapaud	a large toad.
dasheen	a root vegetable.
day clean	early morning when the sun has come up.
dollsup	made up with cosmetics.
douens	a folk spirit of the forest notorious for luring children away from home.
doun	down.
eddoes	a root vegetable.
foreday morning	dawn.
Gaard	God.
gial	girl.
gol-eye sarah	a brown bird, the size of a starling with yellow eyes.
god-horse	a stick insect.
gri-gri	a red berry with a kernel which is delicious.
gundy	a crab's claw.
Hosein	a Muslim festival with the beating of drums.
Jab jab	a traditional masquerade character: a cross between a medieval jester and a clown carrying a long whip.
Jacahuna	Arawak god of manioc.
Jamette	a person of questionable morals.
jeez-an-ages	an exclamation with the accent on 'jeez', usually expressing exasperation or astonishment.
johnny-bakes	a favourite Tobago bread, baked in an iron cooking pot.
jumbie	a spirit, usually mischievous or bad.
jumbie bead	a small red and black bead resembling an eye.
kaiso	calypso.
kiat	cat.
kiskadee	a little bird in Trinidad whose song is very much like the French, *qu'est ce qu'il dit*.
Laard	Lord.
La Diablesse	a character of Trinidad folklore: a beautiful woman whose peculiarity is having a cow

	hoof instead of a left foot. She lures men away and loses them in the forest.
l'école biche	truanting.
Loupgarou	the male counterpart of Soucouyant. (See Soucouyant.)
macajuel	a large snake which swallows its victim whole after crushing it.
macumere	a female friend of many years standing; womanish.
maladie	a sickness.
mal yeux	the evil eye.
mamaguy	a mild form of deception through flattery; to make fun of.
Mama Malade	a folk spirit of a woman who died in childbirth.
manioc	cassava, a root vegetable.
mapepire zanana	one of Trinidad's venomous snakes. It is aggressive when disturbed.
naygar	'nigger', accepted as a humorous endearment only among very good friends. Outside this context it is considered pejorative in the extreme.
to nyam	to eat.
odderhan	other hand.
Papa Bois	a character of Trinidad folklore reputed as a protector of forest animals.
pappyshow	a person of ridicule.
pewah	a fruit of the palm family which is delicious when cooked.
pickney	child.
pickant	thorn.
pomme-arac	a juicy fruit with a magenta red skin and white flesh.
rat	one of the names given to a prostitute. A term used in the 1930s.
rocksage	a wild hardy scrub.
sabot	wooden slippers.

sapodilla	a sweet juicy fruit, greenish-brown of skin.
shango	the ritualistic ceremony dedicated to the Yoruba god of thunder and lightning, Shango.
Soucouyant	a folklore character with the ability to transform herself into a ball of fire and to fly around at night searching for victims whose blood she sucks.
tania	a root vegetable.
washicongs	soft canvas shoes.
yeye	eye.
zandolie	a green ground lizard.
zootie	stinging nettles.

Other poetry titles published by
Bogle-L'Ouverture Publications

TENDER FINGERS IN A CLENCHED FIST by Lemn Sissay. A collection of sixty-one poems that is meant to be performed and Lemn Sissay does just that; whether the poetry is read to you or bouncing off the pages as written words.

A Mancunian by birth but from a tradition centuries old of dramatist and storyteller, Lemn Sissay not only captures the feelings and sounds of his native Manchester in 'The Invasion of the Mancunoids' some of whom ...

> got shoulders you could mistake as Hulme fly-over
> chips as square as the white cliffs of Dover
> pants as tight as a packet of durex

or as in the heightened awareness in 'Gold from the Stone' when he writes that you

> Can't give light to the sun
> Nor a drink, to the sea
> The earth I must stand upon
> I shall kiss with my history.

An indefatigable performer, Lemn has appeared at venues throughout the country and has a regular spot on both BBC and community radio stations in Manchester.

ISBN 0 904 521 44 3 (cloth) £7.95
ISBN 0 904 521 45 1 (paper) £4.95

DREAD BEAT AND BLOOD by Linton Kwesi Johnson is a poetic statement of what it was like to be black and growing up in Britain during the 1970s. Linton's work has been a major influence on the new generation of poets and songwriters searching for both vehicle and validity for what they have to say about the black condition. Now in its fifth edition.

ISBN 0 904 521 06 0   £4.95

EASTER MONDAY BLUES by Accabre Huntley. As in her first volume Accabre's concerns continue to be about her experiences at school. In 'Ten Little Teachers' as well as wider social issues as in 'Charles and Di' the poet reflects a maturity for sustained poetic expressions on a wide range of topics as Accabre, then sixteen, grows in confidence with the rest of the community. This collection is dedicated to all children of the world.

ISBN 0 904 521 23 0   £2.95

JAMAICA: an epic poem, exploring the historical foundations of Jamaican society by Andrew Salkey. A poem about Jamaica, about the experiences of the slave trade, colonialism, and about a struggle for freedom and identity which still rages today among Caribbean peoples. Twenty years in the writing, this epic poem conjures up the swirling colours, the music, the moods, the atmosphere of a bustling, suffering, vital island community.

ISBN 0 904 521 26 5   £4.95

DAYS AND NIGHTS IN THE MAGIC FOREST by Faustin Charles. The title poem is evocative of the spirituality and magic of the Caribbean landscape. The other poems reflect beauty, tragedy and exile. All are concerned with the sense of belonging and strength of faith in the future of the Caribbean. Faustin Charles' previously published collection **Crab Track** is also available.

ISBN 0 904 521 53 2   £4.95
ISBN 0 904 521 40 0   £7.95

WALTER RODNEY: POETIC TRIBUTES compiled and edited by Eric L. Huntley. An anthology of poetry. The poets have contributed works which are variously elegiac, discursive, lyrical and devotional.

Most were spontaneous responses to the murder of the historian and political activist Walter Rodney on June 13th 1980.

The publisher's use of calligraphy by Firdous Ali and an unfinished portrait of Walter Rodney by Errol Lloyd on the cover, makes this anthology a collectors' piece, without a doubt.

ISBN 0 904 521 30 3   £5.95

HOUR OF ASSASSINS AND OTHER POEMS is Cecil Rajendra's sixth volume of poetry. The collection shows his concern about man and his future, the murder of his friend and comrade Walter Rodney, to whom the book is dedicated, the birth of his baby daughter, the rubber tappers of his island home, the bombing of Lebanese towns by Israeli forces, the concern for preservation of the earth's natural beauty and resources and its wanton plundering. Cecil is one of the 'finest' and most 'fearless' poets writing in Asia today.

ISBN 0 904 521 29 X   £3.95

CHILD OF THE SUN by Cecil Rajendra. Cecil Rejendra is one of Malaysia's most prolific writers of poetry and is most respected and well known. His poetry spans a writing career of many years as well as the subjects and themes which range over a wide spectrum of human concerns, from love to ecology. His poems have been translated into several languages including Urdu, German, Chinese, Japanese and Malay.

ISBN 0 904 521 37 0   £4.95

SECRET LIVES by Imruh Bakari, seeks to map out and

explore the experience of West Indian peoples migration to Britain and the trauma of coming to terms with it; then to evoke some kind of liberation. Imruh is inspired by the oral speech patterns of the Caribbean and the various performing arts, particularly music.

ISBN 0 904 521 3 62   £4.95
ISBN 0 904 521 35 4   £6.95

TOUCH MI TELL MI by Valerie Bloom. One of the many new voices writing in the rich oral tradition of the Caribbean.
Whether she is writing about everyday occurrences of village life, major issues such as nuclear power or the discomfort of the British winter. Valerie's poetry entertains as well as offering insights into the human condition. Now in its second edition.

ISBN 0 904 521 27 3   £5.95
ISBN 0 904 521 45 1   £9.95
ISBN 0 904 521 25 7   £5,95 (cassette)

WAILING THE DEAD TO SLEEP Lucinda Roy. Poetry that is a 'fusion of images which are both physical and concrete and yet have the transience of joy and pain which accompanies the deepest of life's experiences' – Anne Johnson – Lucinda's first published collection is introduced by Nikki Giovanni. 'I like the comfort of Lucinda ... the steady courage she displays ... gathering summer's harvest ... for fall leaves ... to cover'.
Lucinda is Assistant Professor in English and Creative Writing at Virginia State Polytechnic and University, USA.

ISBN 0 904 521 42 7   £7.95
ISBN 0 904 521 43 3   £4.95